D0534945

RECIPES AND PHOTOGRAPHS
SANDRA MAHUT

Unicorn Food

Table of contents

Recipes for happiness

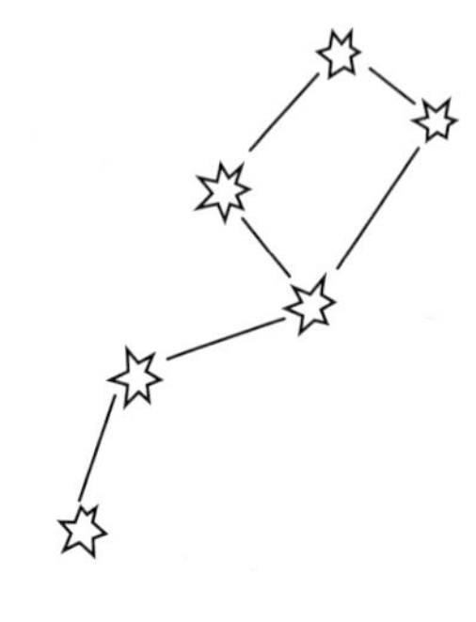

THE PRINCIPLE

We are fascinated by the unicorn—a fantastic, fabulous being! When its colorful universe lands on our plate, we smile. The aim is to eat a rainbow, but a healthy one, thanks to recipes that are both balanced and colorful, that will delight the eyes as well as the taste buds.

We are often wary of conventional food colorings (too many chemicals, potentially harmful to your health, etc.). Natural food colorings allow you to decorate and give originality to your creations just as well as conventional food colorings, but safely. No artificial food colorings are used in this book: they are all plant-based.

The sweet and savory recipes offered here are equally spectacular, to eat as well as look at.

NATURAL FOOD COLORINGS

Many of the products we use every day have powerful coloring properties—colors that can be extracted by boiling, blending, and so on.

This is the case with spinach leaves, beetroot, or carrot juice, but it also applies to spices, such as turmeric and paprika.

To save time, you can use natural powdered food colorings found in specialty cake-decorating shops or on the internet.

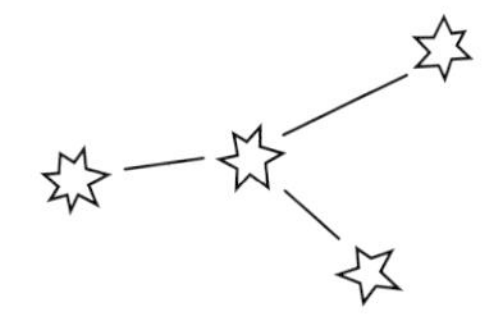

MAKING PRETTY COLORS

Blue: red cabbage juice + lemon; curaçao or natural powdered blue food coloring (blue spirulina, acai, or Klamath Algae); powdered food coloring for cake decorating derived from phycocyanin (a blue pigment contained in a micro algae derived from spirulina)

Purple: blueberry juice; beetroot; acai powder

Mauve: red cabbage juice

Yellow: curry powder; turmeric; bee pollen grains ground to a powder

Orange-yellow: turmeric

Pink/Red: raspberry juice (or the juice of another berry); beetroot juice; hibiscus juice; achiote seeds, infused and mixed with almond milk or cream cheese

Green: green spirulina; spinach juice; matcha; barley grass powder

Orange: carrot juice; sea buckthorn juice; paprika

Mermaid toast

Preparation time: 5 minutes

Makes 4 pieces of toast

4 slices of sandwich bread or square crispbreads
1 cup (200 g) cream cheese
2 to 3 drops each of natural blue, green, and pink food coloring
Raspberry or blackcurrant coulis
1 pinch of blue and green spirulina
1 pinch of edible glitter

Toast the bread.

Keep half of the cream cheese plain and divide the rest into three bowls, using the food coloring to create three different colors of cream cheese.

Spread a layer of plain cream cheese on each slice of toast, top with a layer of colored cream cheese, a few drops of rasberry or blackcurrant coulis, and a sprinkle of blue or green spirulina. Spread with an offset spatula. Sprinkle with edible glitter and serve immediately!

To make them even more fairytale-like, you can add dragon fruit slices cut into flower or star shapes using a cookie cutter or cucumber shapes colored with a drop of blackcurrant coulis.

Unicorn dips

Preparation time: 25 minutes

Serves 4

Hummus

1 tablespoon (15 g) tahini (white sesame paste)
3 tablespoons (50 ml) hot water
2 cups (500 g) canned chickpeas
2 garlic cloves
Juice of 1 lemon
3 tablespoons (50 ml) olive oil
2 teaspoons (5 g) salt
1½ cups (300 g) diced beetroot, cooked
1 teaspoon natural blue powdered food coloring or powdered blue spirulina

Sesame guacamole

2 ripe avocados
2 tablespoons (28 ml) olive oil
Lemon juice
Salt and pepper
1 pinch of green spirulina

Fresh vegetables and sesame seeds for decoration

Making the hummus

Dilute the tahini in 3 tablespoons (50 ml) of hot water. Drain the chickpeas. Cut the garlic cloves in half. Blend together the tahini, chickpeas, garlic, and olive oil in a food processor until you have a very smooth purée. Add salt to taste. Divide the mixture into two portions. Set aside in the refrigerator.

For the pink hummus, blend the cooked beetroot in a food proceesor and mix into one portion of the mixture.

For the blue hummus, mix the natural blue food coloring into the other portion, and then place a drop of liquid blue food coloring in the middle for a guaranteed 'mermaid' effect.

Decorate with stars of carrot, cucumber, or pink radish, cut out with a cookie cutter.

Making the guacamole

Mash all the ingredients or blend in a food processor. Add a little extra olive oil or water to make the guacamole smooth. Check for seasoning.

Top with white sesame seeds and some cucumber stars.

Serve with breadsticks for dipping.

Rainbow veggie sandwich

Preparation time: 20 minutes

Makes 2 sandwiches

4 crispbreads or slices of toasted seeded bread
2 carrots
1 raw beetroot
2 tablespoons (28 ml) olive oil
2 pinches of pink Himalayan salt
1 tomato
1 avocado
½ of a cucumber
½ of a mango
½ of a head of iceberg lettuce
½ cup (50 g) red cabbage
A few pink radishes
2 tablespoons (28 g) grated imitation crabmeat
1 tablespoon (14 g) mayonnaise with 1 drop of natural pink food coloring
¼ cup (50 g) cream cheese
Natural blue food coloring or blue spirulina

Peel and cut the carrots and raw beetroot into matchsticks and place them in separate small bowls. Drizzle them with a little olive oil and add a pinch of pink salt. Let them marinate.

Thinly slice the tomato, avocado, cucumber, mango, iceberg lettuce, red cabbage, and radishes. Mix the grated imitation crabmeat in a bowl with the pink mayonnaise.

Place 2 slices of bread or crispbread on a plate, spread with a little cream cheese, add a little spirulina or natural food coloring, and spread again with the spatula, as for the Mermaid Toast (page 6). Lay on slices of tomato, avocado, cucumber, iceberg lettuce, and mango, then the carrot matchsticks, then a layer of pink mayonnaise, and then the red cabbage, beetroot matchsticks, and radish slices.

Top each sandwich with a slice of bread spread with cream cheese in the same way as the first slice. Wrap the sandwiches tightly in plastic wrap.

Keep in the refrigerator for 1 to 2 hours.

Cut each sandwich in two at serving time.

I BELIEVE IN UNICORNS

Unicorn rice paper rolls

Preparation time: 15 minutes

Makes 6 small rice paper rolls

½ of a packet of cellophane noodles
1 to 2 drops of natural blue food coloring or blue spirulina
1 carrot
1 cucumber
½ a head of red cabbage
A few pink radishes
½ avocado
6 rice paper wrappers
A few green lettuce leaves
Black and white sesame seeds
½ mango for decoration

Lemon coconut tahini sauce
1 tablespoon (15 g) tahini
1 tablespoon (15 ml) sesame oil
Juice of ½ of a lime
1 tablespoon (15 ml) coconut cream
1 teaspoon light soy sauce
1 drop of natural blue food coloring

Cook the cellophane noodles according to the instructions on the packet, adding a little blue food coloring to the cooking water. Once the noodles are colored, set aside in a bowl of cold water. Peel and cut the carrot and half of the cucumber into thin matchsticks. Thinly slice the red cabbage. Slice the radishes into rounds and thinly slice the avocado.

Moisten a sheet of rice paper and place it on a slightly damp, clean tea towel. Cut off the top edge of the wrapper (to give a straight side for an open-ended roll). Arrange the lettuce leaves, noodles, and vegetables in the middle, starting with the ingredients that will show through. Wrap up the roll, using your fingertips to tightly close the lower part.

Place the rolls in the refrigerator. At serving time, sprinkle with black and white sesame seeds and then decorate with stars cut out of the mango or the rest of the cucumber.

Blend the sauce ingredients, except the food coloring, in a food processor. Add the drop of blue food coloring and swirl once with the tip of a knife to make a pretty spiral and then sprinkle with a few sesame seeds. Serve the rolls with the sauce.

Unicorn maki rolls

Preparation time: 20 minutes – Cooking time: 50 minutes – Resting time: 1 night

Makes about 10 pieces of maki (two long rolls)

1 small bamboo mat

½ of a head of romaine lettuce
2 sticks of imitation crabmeat
1 cucumber
1 avocado
Wasabi and sesame seeds
Soy sauce seasoned with a drop of sesame oil and a few black and white sesame seeds

Vinegared rice

¾ cup (150 g) short-grain sushi rice
2 to 3 tablespoons (28 to 45 ml) rice vinegar
1 teaspoon fine salt
1 tablespoon (12 g) superfine sugar
Natural pink, blue, yellow, and purple food coloring

Making the vinegared rice

Cook the rice according to the instructions on the packet. Once cooked, remove the lid of the saucepan and let the rice rest for 10 minutes.

Heat the vinegar, salt, and sugar together in a saucepan and mix to dissolve the sugar and salt, without bringing to a boil. Allow to cool.

Divide the vinegar mixture between four bowls, adding drops of food coloring to each bowl.

Place the rice in a large mixing bowl to cool and then divide it between the bowls of vinegar to make blue, pink, purple, and yellow rice.

Making the maki rolls

Wash and dry the lettuce leaves and cut them into thick, rectangular bands. Place the lettuce bands on the bamboo mat and then lay a line of each colored rice, about ¼ inch (6 mm) thick, to make a sort of rainbow. Place a strip of imitation crabmeat, cucumber, and avocado on top. Roll the rice onto itself with the help of the mat, rolling tightly so it is firm. Repeat the process for the second roll.

Place the rolls in the refrigerator overnight.
The next day, cut them into sections about 1 inch (3 cm) wide. Serve immediately with wasabi and sesame seeds, with the soy and sesame sauce on the side.

Veggie noodle bowl

Preparation time: 40 minutes – Cooking time: 40 minutes – Resting time: 10 minutes

Makes 2 bowls

4 ounces (100 g) cellophane noodles
2 drops of natural blue liquid food coloring
2 drops of natural purple or fuchsia pink food coloring
1 avocado
½ of a dragon fruit
5 pink radishes
½ of a red beetroot
½ of a cucumber
Black and white sesame seeds
A few blue edible flowers (pansy or borage)

Sauce
1 tablespoon (15 g) tahini
1 teaspoon white miso
2 tablespoons (28 ml) lemon juice
1 tablespoon (15 ml) soy sauce
1 pinch of ground ginger
1 tablespoon (15 ml) sesame oil
1 tablespoon (15 ml) coconut milk
1 tablespoon (15 ml) hot water

Make the sauce by mixing all of the ingredients together.

Cook the cellophane noodles according to the instructions on the packets in two saucepans, one with blue food coloring and the other with pink food coloring. Once the noodles are colored, set aside in bowls of cold water.

Drain and arrange the two colored noodles in two bowls and then add thinly sliced avocado and dragon fruit, the radishes cut into rounds, and the raw beetroot and cucumber cut into stars with a cookie cutter. Sprinkle with black and white sesame seeds and edible flowers.

Serve with the sauce poured over the top and mix well before enjoying.

You can, of course, add other kinds of fruit or vegetables to this bowl: halved strawberries, arugula, yellow bell pepper, spring onion, etc.

Preparation time: 10 minutes – Cooking time: 5 minutes

Makes 4 croque-unicorns

1 cup (150 g) grated mozzarella cheese
¾ cup (100 g) grated gruyère cheese
Natural food coloring (4 different colors)
8 slices of white sandwich bread
1½ tablespoons (20 g) butter
4 ounces (120 g) mortadella

Mix the cheeses together and divide between four bowls. Add a few drops of each food coloring and mix to color evenly.

Butter the eight slices of bread on both sides.

Arrange the four colored cheeses on four of the slices of bread in side-by-side strips. Add a slice of mortadella, cover with another layer of colored cheese strips, and top with another slice of bread.

Cook the croque-unicorns, two at a time, in a sandwich toaster for 5 minutes at 350°F (180°C) or in the oven for 5 minutes at 400°F (200°C, or gas mark 6).

Celestial swirl soup

Preparation time: 10 minutes – Cooking time: 30 to 40 minutes

Serves 4

3 cups (400 g) purple carrots
1¾ cups (150 g) red cabbage
1 red onion
1½ tablespoons (20 g) salted butter
3½ cups (800 ml) vegetable stock
Salt and pepper
¾ cup (200 ml) whipping cream
2 pinches of natural blue powdered food coloring (or blue spirulina)
White sesame seeds
Edible blue flowers (such as borage)

Peel the carrots and cut them and the red cabbage into chunks. Finely chop the red onion. Melt the butter in a large saucepan or Dutch oven and add the onion. Sweat the onion and add the carrots and red cabbage. Pour in the stock and season with salt and pepper. Cover and cook for about 30 to 40 minutes.

Blend well in a food processor, adding a little whipping cream.

When serving in bowls, drizzle some whipping cream over top and add some blue food coloring. Sprinkle with white sesame seeds and add a few edible flowers.

Serve immediately.

You can also add some orange or lemon zest.

Rainbow pancakes

Preparation time: 10 minutes – Cooking time: 15 to 20 minutes – Resting time: 30 minutes

Makes 12 pancakes

2 cups (250 g) all-purpose flour
1 pinch of fine salt
¼ cup (50 g) superfine sugar
1 teaspoon vanilla extract
2 teaspoons (10 g) baking powder
2 organic eggs
3 tablespoons (50 ml) sunflower or grapeseed oil
⅔ cup (150 ml) whole milk
Natural food coloring (green, blue, yellow, and pink)
2 ounces (60 g) white chocolate candy melts
Colored edible decorations for sprinkling
Coconut flakes

Mix together the flour, salt, sugar, vanilla extract, and baking powder in a mixing bowl. Add the eggs, one at a time, whisking with a fork. Add the oil and whisk again. Pour in the milk and whisk until the batter is quite smooth.

Divide the batter between three or four bowls (depending on the number of colors), add a little natural food coloring to each, mix well, and let the batter stand at room temperature for 30 minutes.

Pour a small ladleful of batter into a hot, greased skillet, turning over each pancake when bubbles appear. Stack the cooked pancakes on a plate. Melt the white chocolate candy melts in a double boiler. Pour the melted white chocolate over the pancakes. Decorate and sprinkle with coconut flakes.

Blueberry galaxy cupcakes

Preparation time: 1 hour – Cooking time: 25 minutes – Resting time: 1 hour

Makes 6 to 7 cupcakes

1 cup (130 g) all-purpose flour
½ cup (80 g) sugar
1 teaspoon baking powder
1 pinch of salt
1 egg
⅓ cup (70 ml) milk
2 tablespoons (28 ml) sunflower oil
¾ cup (100 g) blueberries
Edible decorations: silver, blue, star-shaped, etc.

Frosting

2 tablespoons (25 g) unsalted butter, softened
½ cup (110 g) cream cheese
½ cup (50 g) confectioner's sugar
¼ cup (50 g) mascarpone cheese
Natural food coloring (dark blue, light blue, and purple)

Preheat the oven to 350°F (180°C, or gas mark 4).

Mix together the flour, sugar, baking powder, and salt in a large mixing bowl.

Beat the egg in another mixing bowl and then add the milk and oil. Incorporate the dry mixture into the wet mixture and then add the blueberries, mixing very gently so you don't damage them. Divide the batter between paper baking cups.

Bake for 20 minutes. Remove from the oven and let the cupcakes cool on a rack for 30 minutes before decorating them.

Frosting & decoration

Beat the softened butter with the cream cheese in a mixing bowl with an electric hand mixer. Make sure it is quite smooth and then add the confectioner's sugar and mascarpone. Beat the mixture for a few minutes until it is very smooth.

Divide this mixture between three bowls. Add a few drops of food coloring to each bowl. Mix each color separately so they are quite different.

Fill one piping bag with the three colored frostings. Place the bag in the refrigerator for 30 minutes. Pipe frosting onto each cupcake, pressing gently and making circles. Decorate the cupcakes.

The cupcakes will keep for 2 days in the refrigerator in an airtight container.

Rainbow cupcakes

Preparation time: 1 hour – Cooking time: 25 minutes – Resting time: 1 hour

Makes 6 cupcakes

6 tablespoons (85 g) softened butter
½ cup (100 g) superfine sugar
1 egg
1 cup (130 g) all-purpose flour
1 teaspoon vanilla extract
1 teaspoon baking powder
1 pinch of salt
6 tablespoons (90 ml) milk
⅓ cup (50 g) strawberries
Paper unicorns sugar decorations

Frosting

2 tablespoons (25 g) butter
½ cup (110 g) cream cheese
¼ cup (50 g) confectioner's sugar
¼ cup (50 g) mascarpone cheese
A few drops of natural food coloring (blue, pink, green, yellow, and purple)
A little cotton candy to decorate

Preheat the oven to 350°F (180°C, or gas mark 4).

Beat the butter with the sugar in a mixing bowl and then add the egg.

In another mixing bowl, mix together the flour, vanilla, baking powder, and salt. Then, stir half of this dry mixture into the wet mixture. Add half of the milk and beat. Add the other half of the dry mixture and milk and beat until the batter is smooth and well combined.

Fill six paper baking cups three quarters full and bake for 20 to 25 minutes. Remove from the oven and allow to cool for 30 minutes before decorating.

Once cooled, remove a teaspoon of cake from the middle of each cupcake and push half a strawberry into the hole (or a whole strawberry if it is small).

Frosting & decoration

Follow the instructions for making the frosting on page 24.

Divide this mixture between five bowls and add a few drops of blue, pink, purple, yellow, and green food coloring to each bowl. Mix in each color well with a soft spatula. Fill the one piping bag with all the frosting colors.

Once the cupcakes have cooled, make rainbows with the multicolored frosting in the piping bag. Top with a piece of cotton candy and decorate with a paper unicorn or a horn made from fondant icing.

Cosmic donuts

Preparation time: 30 min – Cooking time: 20 minutes – Resting time: 1 hour 30 mins + 1 hour drying time

Makes 6 donuts

0.1 ounce (3 g) cake yeast
6 tablespoons (90 ml) lukewarm water (68°F, or 20°C)
1¼ cups (140 g) all-purpose flour

1 tablespoon (15 ml) milk
0.7 onces (20 g) cake yeast, additional
2 tablespoons (30 g) sugar
1 cup (125 g) all-purpose flour
4 egg yolks
1 teaspoon (5 g) salt
2 tablespoons (30 g) softened butter
1 quart (1 L) oil for deep frying
Edible silver glitter, metallic sugar pearls, etc.

Icing
1 egg white
1⅓ cups (250 g) confectioner's sugar
1 squeeze of lemon juice
Natural blue food coloring

Crumble the yeast, pour over the lukewarm water to dissolve it, add the flour, and mix together. Form into a ball and let it rise in a warm but turned-off oven for 1 hour.

Place this starter in a mixing bowl or the bowl of a stand mixer. Work the dough with your fists or use the kneading setting for 3 minutes and then add the milk while continuing to knead.

Stir in the additional crumbled yeast and then the sugar, flour, egg yolks, and salt. Work the dough for 3 minutes. It should be very smooth. Add the softened butter. Shape into a ball and cover with plastic wrap. Let it rise for 1 hour. The dough should double in volume.

Divide the dough into 6 portions. Make a hole in the middle with your finger and then widen the hole to give it a donut shape.

Place the donuts on a baking sheet lined with parchment paper and let them rise for at least 30 minutes at room temperature. Deep fry them in the oil at 350°F (180°C) for 3 minutes on each side. Drain and place on paper towels.

Icing & decoration
Using a fork, mix together the egg white, confectioner's sugar, and lemon juice in a bowl. When the icing is smooth, add the blue food coloring (spirulina will give a wonderful blue). Spread the icing on each donut and let it dry for 1 hour.

Unicorn selfie cookies

Preparation time: 30 minutes – Cooking time: 8 minutes – Resting time: 1 hour

Makes about 30 cookies

1 cup (230 g) softened butter
1 cup (200 g) superfine sugar
1 egg
1 teaspoon vanilla extract
3 cups (375 g) all-purpose flour
1 teaspoon (5 g) baking powder
Edible gold glitter or gel
Black icing pen

Icing
1 egg white
2 teaspoons (10 ml) lemon juice
2 cups (250 g) confectioner's sugar
Natural food colorings

Beat the softened butter and sugar together using an electric hand mixer. Add the egg and the vanilla. Stir in the flour and baking powder. Shape the dough into a ball. Wrap in plastic wrap and set aside in the refrigerator for at least 1 hour.

Preheat the oven to 350°F (180°C, or gas mark 4).

Roll out the cold dough to a thickness of around ¼ inch (6 mm). Cut unicorn, cloud, and/or star shapes out of the dough using a cookie cutter. Place the cookies on a baking sheet lined with parchment paper. Place the tray in the refrigerator for a few minutes. Remove from the refrigerator and bake for 8 minutes. Take out of the oven and cool.

Icing & decoration
Mix the egg white, lemon juice, and sugar together. The icing should be a little thick to start with, so that it stays within the shapes. Adjust the consistency by adding more confectioner's sugar or water.

Divide into as many bowls as you have colors (remembering to leave one as white) and then add the colorings to each bowl.

Spread the icing on the shapes. To make the unicorn's mane, pipe lines of different colors. Let the icing dry for a few minutes after each line. You can add a little water (very little at a time) to make the icing more liquid if it dries too quickly. Let it dry for at least 1 hour.

Decorate the horn of the unicorn with edible gold glitter or gel and draw in the eyes with the icing pen.

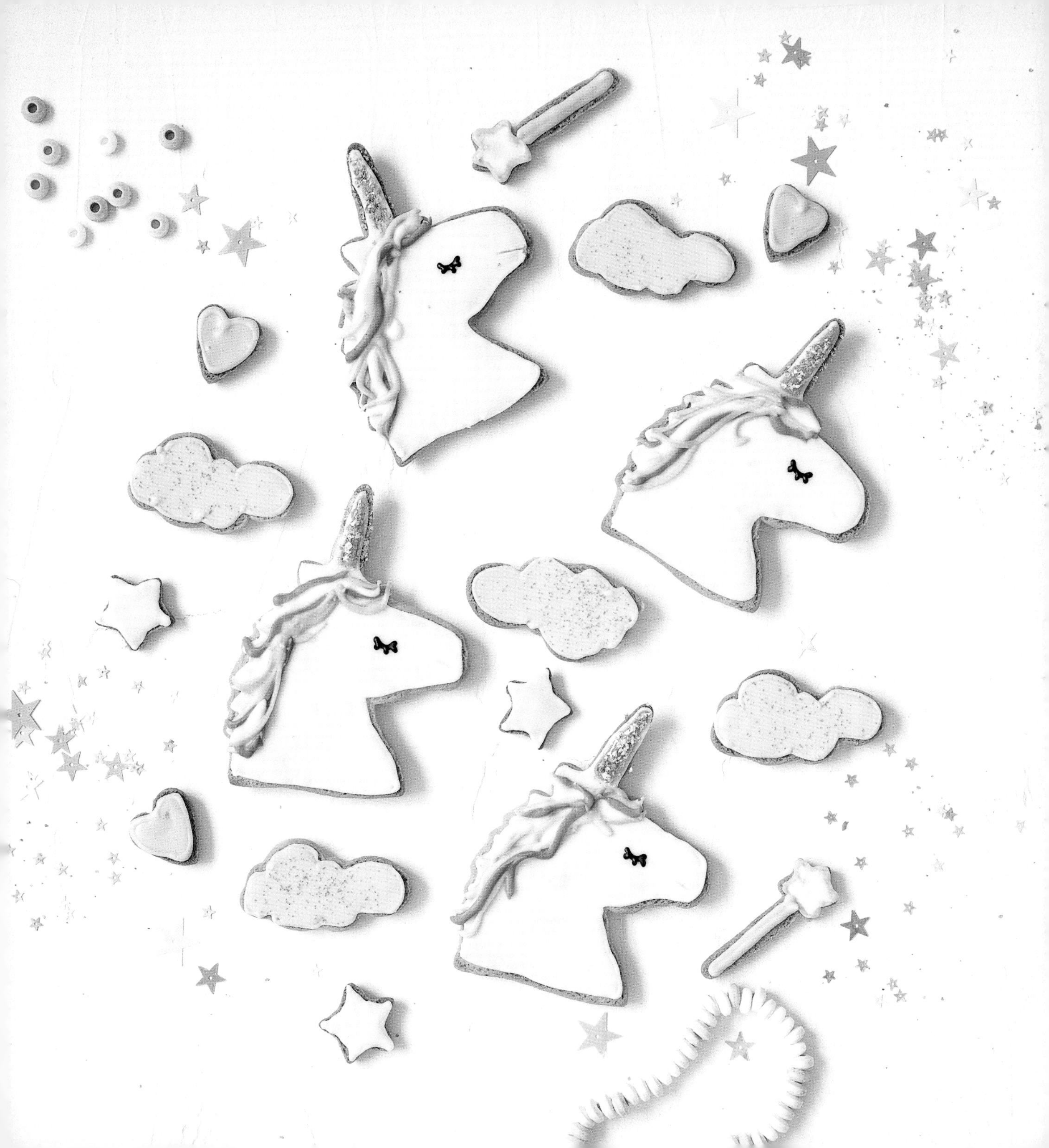

Unicorn poop

Preparation time: 15 minutes – Cooking time: 1 hour

¼ cup (60 g) egg whites (2 eggs)
⅔ cup (120 g) superfine sugar
Natural pink, green, and blue food coloring

Preheat the oven to 225°F (110°C, or gas mark ¼).

Beat the egg whites to stiff peaks. At the moment they start to thicken, add the sugar while continuing to beat.

Divide the mixture between four bowls. Leave one bowl white and add drops of coloring to the remaining three bowls.

Lay a rectangle of plastic wrap on a flat surface. Place half the contents of one bowl into a piping bag without a nozzle. Pipe the mixture in a line on the plastic wrap. Using half the mixture from another bowl, pipe another line next to the first. Repeat this process until you have used all the mixture and have eight lines of alternating colors. Roll the plastic wrap onto itself without closing the ends and place it in a piping bag with a star nozzle.

Pipe the meringues onto a baking sheet covered with a sheet of parchment paper, spacing them well apart. Bake for 1 hour.

When they come out of the oven, place the meringues on a rack to cool and enjoy.

The meringues will keep in an airtight container for up to 1 week.

Unicorn dessert bars

Preparation time: 30 minutes – Cooking time: 25 to 30 minutes – Resting time: 1 hour

Makes one 16 x 14 inch (40 x 35 cm) tray (for about 10 people)

⅔ cup (150 g) softened butter
1 cup (200 g) superfine sugar
1 pinch of salt
3 eggs
½ teaspoon vanilla extract
2¼ cups (300 g) all-purpose flour
3 tablespoons (40 g) colored sugar decoration: sprinkles, edible confetti, stars, etc.

Frosting

3 tablespoons (40 g) softened butter
½ cup (110 g) cream cheese
½ cup (50 g) confectioner's sugar
1 to 2 teaspoons (5 to 10 ml) natural blue food coloring

Start by making the frosting. Beat the butter until creamy and then add the cream cheese until the mixture is well combined. Add the confectioner's sugar and food coloring and beat the mixture until smooth.

Place this mixture into a piping bag fitted with a star or plain nozzle. Place the bag in the refrigerator for 1 hour.

Preheat the oven to 350°F (180°C, or gas mark 4).

Beat the butter with the sugar and salt to make the batter. Add the eggs, one at a time, and then the vanilla. Beat continuously and then add the flour. Beat until the mixture is smooth.

Add most of the sugar decorations and mix through with a spatula. The batter should be quite thick and full of decorations. Spread this batter in a swiss roll pan to a thickness of ½ inch (1 cm). Bake for 25 to 30 minutes.

When it comes out of the oven, let cool on a rack. Once it has completely cooled, pipe small spirals of frosting on top, about 1 inch (2 or 3 cm) in diameter, and sprinkle with the remaining sugar decorations.

Cut into small squares to serve.

Unicorn cheesecake

Preparation time: 30 minutes – Refrigeration: 1 day – Resting time: 1 hour

Serves 6

8 ounces (200 g) graham crackers
6 tablespoons (90 g) butter
1¼ cup (300 g) Greek-style yogurt
2½ cups (600 g) cream cheese
1 tablespoon (15 ml) lemon juice
½ cup (125 ml) water
⅓ cup (75 g) superfine sugar
2 gelatin sheets
3 or 4 different natural food colorings

Crush the graham crackers in a sealed zip top bag using a rolling pin.

Melt the butter in a microwave oven. Pour the melted butter over the crushed graham crackers and work together to form a grainy dough. Use it to line the bottom of a 10-inch (26 cm) springform cake pan, pushing it up the sides a little by pressing a glass around the edge. Set aside in the refrigerator for 1 hour.

Mix the yogurt with the cream cheese and lemon juice. Beat with a whisk for 2 minutes.

Boil the water in a saucepan with the sugar to make a syrup. Once dissolved, turn off the heat and add the gelatin, rehydrated in water beforehand. Mix well so that the gelatin completely dissolves. Pour into the yogurt and cream cheese mixture and whisk well so the mixture is combined.

Divide the mixture between three or four bowls. Add a food coloring to each bowl and mix to make pastel shades.

Remove the cheesecake base from the refrigerator and add the colored fillings to the pan. Place one color on top of another until all the filling is used.

Trace spirals through the filling with a wooden skewer and place in the refrigerator for 24 hours. Unmold and serve immediately.

Swiss roll

Preparation time: 25 minutes – Cooking time: 10 minutes – Resting time: 10 to 30 minutes

Serves 10

Sponge cake

4 eggs
⅔ cup (125 g) sugar
1 teaspoon vanilla extract
1 cup (125 g) all-purpose flour

Filling

⅔ cup (150 g) cream cheese
1¼ cups (300 g) mascarpone cheese
½ cup (60 g) confectioner's sugar
Juice of 1 lemon
1 teaspoon natural blue food coloring (such as blue spirulina or Klamath Algae)
¾ cup (100 g) small, round strawberries
Sparkly sugar decorations in blue, pink, purple, paper unicorns etc.

Place a sheet of parchment paper on a baking sheet. Oil lightly. Preheat the oven to 350°F (180°C, or gas mark 4).

Separate the eggs. Beat the egg yolks with the sugar and vanilla in a mixing bowl until pale and fluffy. Set aside.

In a second mixing bowl, beat the egg whites to stiff peaks. Fold some of the whites into the egg yolk mixture and whisk to loosen the mixture. Fold in the rest of the egg whites. Add the flour in two stages and mix.

Once the mixture is combined, pour onto the prepared baking sheet. Spread out with a spatula and bake for 10 minutes.

Turn over onto a clean, damp tea towel. Lift up the tray and then remove the parchment paper. Trim around the cake so the edges are sharp. Roll it up carefully in the damp tea towel. Let it rest for 10 to 30 minutes.

Prepare the filling by mixing the cream cheese with the mascarpone, confectioner's sugar, and lemon juice. Add the food coloring and mix in.

Unroll the sponge cake and spread it with the blue filling and then scatter with slices of strawberry. Roll up the cake again with the help of the damp tea towel. Spread the rest of the filling over the whole surface of the swiss roll. Decorate with sparkly sugar decorations. Serve immediately or place in the refrigerator.

Rainbow tiramisu

Preparation time: 35 minutes – Resting time: 1 night (at least 4 hours)

Makes 6 tiramisus

3 eggs
¾ cup (80 g) confectioner's sugar
1 teaspoon vanilla extract
1 cup (250 g) mascarpone cheese
1 pinch of salt
½ cup (100 g) frozen raspberries
3 tablespoons (50 ml) water
5 ounces (150 g) pink lady fingers
Fondant icing in different colors for the horn
Whipped cream, for decorating
Sugar decorations: purple, pink, blue, and green edible glitter

Separate the eggs. Beat the sugar, egg yolks, and vanilla in a mixing bowl with an electric hand mixer until creamy. Add the mascarpone and beat again until smooth.

Beat the egg whites with a pinch of salt. When they form firm peaks, fold them gently into the mascarpone cream with a spatula.

Blend the frozen raspberries with a little water in a blender to make a coulis. Cut the pink lady fingers in half and dip them in the raspberry coulis.

Place the lady fingers in six tall glasses, drizzle with coulis (1 to 2 tablespoons [15 to 28 ml]), and then add some mascarpone cream. Repeat the coulis and mascarpone layers.

Place the glasses in the refrigerator overnight (or for at least 4 hours).

To make the sugar horns, roll out balls of fondant icing to make small ropes. Taking two ropes of different colors, wind them around a small wooden skewer. Place the horns in the refrigerator.

At serving time, top with whipped cream and edible glitter. Plant a sugar horn on top and serve.

You can also brush some edible gold glitter mixed with a little water onto the horns.

Unicorn cake

Preparation time: 3 hours – Cooking time: 15 minutes – Resting time: 30 minutes

Serves 6 to 8

Lime sponge cake
5 eggs
¾ cup (155 g) sugar
1 teaspoon vanilla extract
1¼ cups (155 g) all-purpose flour
Zest of 1 lime

Swiss meringue butter cream
5 egg whites
1⅓ cups (250 g) supwerfine sugar
¾ cup (190 g) softened butter

Assembly
Black and white fondant icing
½ cup (100 g) fresh raspberries
Natural food coloring (yellow, green, blue, and pink)
Edible gold glitter or gold sugar pearls for decoration

Preheat the oven to 350°F (180°C, or gas mark 4). Butter and flour 4 small round cake pans, 6 inches (16 cm) in diameter.

Separate the eggs. Beat the egg yolks with the sugar and vanilla in a large bowl until pale and fluffy. Beat the egg whites to soft peaks in a separate bowl. Whisk some of the whites into the first mixture and then gently fold in the rest with a soft spatula. Add the flour and whisk again. Add the lime zest.

Divide the mixture evenly between the cake pans. Smooth the tops with the soft spatula. Bake the cakes for about 10 minutes. They should be lightly golden, but not brown.

Let them cool in the pan for a few minutes and then turn out the cakes while they are still quite hot. Let them cool on a rack in a single layer.

Make the swiss meringue. Heat the egg whites and superfine sugar in a metal bowl over a saucepan of simmering water, beating with an electric hand mixer on medium speed. Increase the speed gradually, until the mixture reaches approximately 122°F (50°C).

Pour the mixture into another bowl, off the saucepan, and continue to beat until completely cooled. The meringue must be smooth, supple and shiny.

Recipe continued on next page

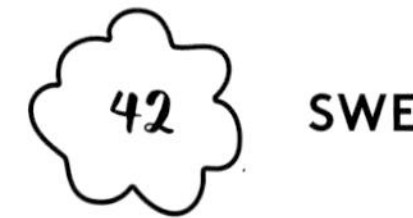

Unicorn cake

continued

Take 2/3 of this mixture and incorporate the softened butter while continuing to beat for 3 minutes. The texture should be firm and creamy. Set aside the swiss meringue butter cream in the refrigerator for 30 minutes. Also set aside the remaining 1/3 of the swiss meringue in the refrigerator, to make the mane later.

Make the eyes, ears, and the horn of the unicorn out of the fondant icing.

Start assembling the cake. Spread a layer of butter cream over a first round of cake, arrange a few raspberries on top, top with a second round of cake, and press down lightly. Repeat the process and finish with the last cake round.

Next, cover the whole cake with a first layer of butter cream and set it aside in the refrigerator for about 10 to 15 minutes. Cover with a second layer of butter cream and smooth the surface. The cake must be very even. If needed, refrigerate for 10 minutes and cover with a final layer of butter cream.

Take out the remaining swiss meringue that was set aside for the mane. Divide between 5 bowls, leave one white and color the others with yellow, green, blue, and pink coloring, whisking in each color well.

Make 5 strips of color side by side on a piece of plastic wrap, roll up, and place inside a piping bag with your choice of nozzle. (See more detailed instructions on page 32.) Set aside in the refrigerator.

Plant the horn and ears on top of the cake and then pipe the rainbow meringue all around the horn and ears, making a mane that goes down the back of the cake and comes back around the side. Arrange the eyes on the side. Sprinkle with edible gold glitter or gold sugar pearls.

Supernova popcorn

Preparation time: 20 minutes – Cooking time: 20 minutes

Serves 4

2 tablespoons (28 ml) grapeseed or sunflower oil
½ cup (150 g) popping corn
½ cup (125 g) water
⅔ cup (125 g) superfine sugar
½ cup (60 g) unsalted butter
Natural food coloring (pink, blue, and green)

Heat the oil for 2 minutes in a large saucepan over medium-high heat. Add the popping corn, cover, and let the kernels pop for about 5 minutes, shaking from time to time to prevent burning.

Bring the water and sugar to a boil in a small saucepan. When a syrup has formed, add the butter. Lower the heat and cook for 5 minutes, mixing well.

Pour the syrup into three small bowls. Add a few drops of food coloring to each bowl and mix in. Add popcorn to each bowl to color it.

Let the popcorn dry at room temperature for a few hours in a dry place or place the bowls in the oven for 5 minutes at 325°F (160°C, or gas mark 3) to dry the popcorn more quickly.

Unicorn macarons

Preparation time: 30 minutes – Cooking time: 15 minutes – Resting time: 1 hour 30 minutes – Refrigeration time: 1 night

Makes 20 macarons

5 ounces (140 g) egg whites (4 eggs)
1 cup (185 g) sugar
1⅓ cups (160 g) extra-fine ground almonds (specially for macarons)
1¼ cups (160 g) confectioner's sugar, sifted
1 teaspoon vanilla extract
Your choice of flavoring (strawberry, rosewater, violet, etc.)
Natural powdered food colorings (Do not use liquid colorings.)
5 ounces (150 g) blue candy melts
2 ounces (50 g) white chocolate candy melts
6 tablespoons (100 ml) whipping cream
1 teaspoon vanilla extract
Gold food paint (or edible gold glitter mixed with water)
Fondant icing for the horn (two colors)

Use an electric hand mixer to beat the egg whites and then add half of the sugar. Continue beating until peaks form and then add the remaining sugar, increasing the speed. Whisk until all of the sugar is dissolved.

Sift the ground almonds and confectioner's sugar into a mixing bowl and fold them gently into the beaten egg whites. Add the vanilla and chosen flavoring.

Separate the mixture into two or three bowls, depending on the number of colors you want. Add one teaspoon of food coloring to each bowl. Preheat the oven to 300°F (150°C, or gas mark 2).

Place spoonfuls of the colored mixtures on top of each other in a piping bag. Pipe the macarons onto a sheet of parchment paper on a baking sheet. Pipe small, uniform rounds. Let them stand for 1 hour in a very dry place. A crust will form on the macarons.

Bake the tray of macarons for 15 minutes. Remove from the oven and allow to cool.

Melt the blue and white chocolate candy melts in a double boiler and mix with a spatula until smooth. Bring the whipping cream to a boil with the vanilla and pour it over the chocolate. Mix until smooth with a spatula.

Place the ganache in the refrigerator for 30 minutes. Pipe the filling on the macaron shells using a plain nozzle and top with another shell. Dab a little gold paint onto each macaron and insert a horn made out of fondant icing in the side.

Unicorn white chocolate bars

Preparation time: 10 minutes – Cooking time: 5 minutes – Resting time: 1 night

Makes 4 bars

14 ounces (400 g) white chocolate candy melts
6 ounces (180 g) blue, pink or purple candy melts
1 ounce (30 g) multicolored sugar decorations
4 plastic chocolate bar molds

Melt the white chocolate and colored candy melts separately in a double boiler. Drizzle spirals of the colored candy melts from a spoon into the bottom of the chocolate bar molds and sprinkle with decorations. Pour the white chocolate over the top. Place in the refrigerator overnight.

Unmold the chocolate bars and sprinkle again with multicolored decorations.

Enjoy with a Unicorn Hot White Chocolate (recipe page 68).

Unicorn ice cream

Preparation time: 20 min – Freezing time : 1 night

Makes a 1 quart (1 L) container of ice cream

1 quart (1 L) whipping cream
3 drops of vanilla extract or
1 vanilla bean
⅔ cup (200 g) sweetened
condensed milk
Natural blue, pink, yellow, purple,
and green food coloring
Multicolored sugar decorations

Beat the whipping cream with the vanilla in a large mixing bowl. When the whipped cream is firm, add the condensed milk and beat again.

Divide this mixture into five small individual bowls. Add a few drops of food coloring to each bowl and gently mix in until you have the color you want.

Pour the contents of the five bowls one by one into a 8 × 4 × 2½-inch (20 × 10 × 6 cm) loaf pan, so the colors are on top of each other. Trace figure eights with a wooden skewer to mix the colors. Sprinkle with decorations and place the pan in the freezer overnight.

The next day, take the pan out 15 minutes before scooping the ice cream.

Multicolored smoothie popsicles

Preparation time: 20 minutes – Freezing time: at least 1 night

Makes 10 popsicles

Blueberries
Strawberries
Blackberries
Mango
Passionfruit
Dragon fruit
½ cup (80 g) sugar or ¼ cup (80 g) agave syrup
3½ cups (800 g) plain yogurt
A few drops of natural food colorings or blue spirulina
1 silicone popsicle mold with 10 wooden popsicle sticks

Cut the fruit into slices or pieces and divide them between bowls according to color. Set a few slices of fruit aside for decoration.

Add the sugar or agave syrup to the yogurt. Leave half of the yogurt plain and mix the remainder with the food colorings to create several different colors.

Place the pieces of fruit in the bottom of the molds and then pour in a little plain yogurt. Finish filling the popsicle molds with different colors of yogurt. Each popsicle should have its own color.

Place in the freezer for at least over night.

Gently unmold and enjoy right away!

Unicorn frozen yogurt bites

Preparation time: 10 minutes – Freezing time: 1 night (at least 4 hours)

Serves 4

1 silicone tray with heart- or star-shaped slots (or an ice cube tray)

1¼ cups (300 g) Greek-style yogurt
2 tablespoons (30 g) sugar or 1½ tabelspoons honey
2 teaspoons (10 ml) vanilla extract
Your choice of natural food colorings (at least three)
Some strips of rainbow candy

Whisk the yogurt with the sugar and vanilla. Divide the mixture between as many bowls as you would like colors.

Add the colorings to each bowl and then mix in until you have the color you want.

Fill a piping bag without a nozzle with spoonfuls of yogurt in each color, layering on top of one other. Fill the slots in the tray. The colors will mix.

Place the bites in the freezer overnight.

Unmold the bites and top each with a piece of rainbow candy to decorate.

Starlight smoothie bowl

Preparation time: 15 minutes

Makes 2 bowls

5 ounces (150 ml) almond milk
3 ounces (100 ml) coconut milk
½ cup (125 g) plain or vanilla yogurt
1 banana
⅓ cup (50 g) blueberries
2 tablespoons (40 g) agave syrup
Natural blue food coloring
1 handful of blackberries
2 tablespoons (30 g) frozen raspberries
A few coconut flakes
½ of a kiwifruit
3 slices of dragon fruit
Edible gold glitter

Pour the almond milk, coconut milk, and yogurt into a blender. Add the banana, sliced into rounds, blueberries (set a few aside for decoration), agave syrup, and the blue food coloring. Blend until you get a nice blue and creamy smoothie.

Pour into two bowls and then decorate with the remaining blueberries, blackberries, crumbled frozen raspberries, coconut flakes, and kiwifruit and dragon fruit cut into stars with a cookie cutter.

Sprinkle with edible gold glitter and serve immediately.

You can add other superfoods to this smoothie, such as acai, maca powder, or hulled hemp seeds.

Blue latté

Preparation time: 5 minutes – Cooking time: 1 minute

Makes 2 glasses

7 ounces (200 ml) almond, oat, or rice milk
2 ounces (50 ml) coconut milk
1 teaspoon ground ginger
Juice of ½ of a lemon
2 teaspoons (15 g) agave syrup
Natural blue food coloring (or blue spirulina or Klamath Algae)
Edible glitter, to decorate
Edible flowers, to decorate

Blend all the ingredients except the edible glitter in a blender. Heat in the microwave or serve cold.

Pour into glasses or mugs.

Sprinkle with edible glitter and edible flowers.

Banana raspberry frappé

Preparation time: 15 minutes

Makes 2 glasses

Blue coulis

2 ounces (60 g) white chocolate melts

2 tablespoons (28 ml) coconut cream

A few drops of natural blue food coloring (or use candy melts that are already colored)

Pink smoothie

6 tablespoons (100 ml) almond milk or reduced fat milk

2 bananas, sliced into rounds and frozen

½ cup (100 g) frozen raspberries

1 tablespoon (15 ml) grenadine or strawberry syrup

½ of a dragon fruit

4 tablespoons (16 g) whipped coconut cream

Pink and blue edible decorations

For the blue coulis, melt the white chocolate candy melts in a double boiler and then add the coconut cream and mix to a smooth and creamy coulis. Add the blue food coloring and mix again. Set aside.

For the pink smoothie, blend the almond milk with the frozen bananas and raspberries in a blender. Add the grenadine or strawberry syrup and the dragon fruit cut into chunks and blend again. Adjust the consistency: add almond milk or water if the smoothie is too thick to drink through a straw.

Make spirals of blue chocolate coulis around the sides of two tall glasses and pour in the pink smoothie. Top with whipped cream and decorate. Serve immediately.

You can also top with some raspberry coulis or more blue coulis.

Rainbow smoothies

Preparation time: 20 minutes

Makes 2 large glasses or jars

5 strawberries
3 bananas
A few raspberries
⅓ cup (50 g) other berries
⅓ cup (50 g) blueberries or blackberries
1 kiwifruit
½ of a mango
6 tablespoons (100 ml) pineapple juice
1 cup (250 g) Greek-style yogurt
½ of a dragon fruit
Edible decorations

The day before, cut up and freeze all the fruits in plastic bags (or use already frozen fruits).

At serving time, blend the strawberries, 2 tablespoons (20 g) of banana, 2 tablespoons (28 ml) of pineapple juice, and 2 tablespoons (30 g) Greek yogurt in a blender and then pour into a large glass or jar. Repeat the process with the same quantity of banana, pineapple juice, and yogurt, each time adding, in turn, the raspberries and other berries, blueberries, kiwifruit, and the mango, to make several layers of color.

Finish by decorating the smoothie, adding a pretty straw and a slice of dragon fruit cut into a star or a few blueberries.

Serve immediately or screw on the lid of the jar to take to the office or a picnic.

Galaxy mocktails

Preparation time: 5 minutes – Freezing time: 6 hours

Makes 4 mocktails

1 quart (1 L) bottle of lemonade
3 tablespoons (50 ml) grenadine syrup
2 limes
A few drops of blue food coloring
4 maraschino cherries
Purple sugar

Pour half of the bottle of lemonade into a baking pan. Place in the freezer for 3 hours and then scrape with a fork to make crystals. Return to the freezer for 3 hours and scrape the granita again. If it is still not frozen enough, place in the freezer for another hour.

Pour a measure of grenadine into each glass. Fill to the rim with granita. Slice the limes into rounds. Place them against the sides of each glass. Pour in the rest of the lemonade and then a few drops of food coloring. Add a maraschino cherry. Sprinkle with purple sugar.

Serve immediately!

MASON

Unicorn hot white chocolate

Preparation time: 10 minutes – Cooking time: 5 minutes

Makes 2 cups

3½ ounces (100 g) white chocolate candy melts
A few drops of natural pink food coloring (or use candy melts that are already colored)
1 cup (250 ml) whole or reduced fat milk
1 tablespoon (15 ml) vanilla extract or a tablespoon (15 ml) grenadine syrup
Whipped cream
A few mini marshmallows

Horns

2 ounces (50 g) white chocolate for melting
Natural blue food coloring
2 ice cream cones
Edible glitter

For the horns, melt a few white chocolate candy melts with some blue food coloring in a double boiler, mixing together well. Cut 2 inches (5 cm) off the top of the cones to make mini-horns. Dip them quickly in the melted blue chocolate and then in the edible glitter. Place in the freezer for 1 hour.

For the hot chocolate, melt the white chocolate candy melts in the double boiler with the pink food coloring, mixing well.

Heat the milk in a saucepan and then pour it over the melted pink chocolate in the double boiler. Beat with a hand whisk. Add the vanilla or grenadine syrup and mix again. The hot chocolate should be very smooth and creamy.

Pour the hot chocolate into cups and top with whipped cream. Sprinkle with mini marshmallows and top with the unicorn horns.

Serve immediately.

Unicorn milkshakes

Preparation time: 15 minutes

Makes 2 large glasses

1 cup (250 ml) reduced fat milk
3½ cups (500 g) vanilla ice cream
Natural pink, blue, yellow, purple, and green food coloring
A few marshmallow twists to decorate
A few sugar decorations: sprinkles, multicolored edible confetti, etc.

Blend the cold milk with the ice cream in a blender for 30 seconds.

Pour the mixture into five bowls and add a different food coloring to each bowl. Mix quickly with a whisk or fork. Pour a little of each color into tall glasses. The colors will mix and form a rainbow.

Serve immediately with the marshmallows, multicolored decorations, and gold straws.

Acknowledgements

I would especially like to thank Juliette Garnier for her talent, accuracy, and help with making the recipes.

I would also like to thank Jennifer for helping me to find, from the other side of the Atlantic, very 'unicorn' ideas and products.

Thanks to Olivier for his daily company, support, and talent as a retoucher!

Thanks to Marabout and Claudie Souchet for their support and enthusiasm for this wonderful project.

To help you with decorations and to make beautiful colors, here are some essential sites:

- www.fancysprinkles.com
- www.scrapcooking.fr/en
- www.essentialingredient.com.au
- www.cakerswarehouse.com.au
- www.countrykitchensa.com
- www.layercakeshop.com
- www.fancyflours.com

Published in 2017 by Murdoch Books, an imprint of Allen & Unwin
First published by Hachette Livre (Marabout) 2017

First Published in the USA in 2018 by Quarry Books,
an imprint of The Quarto Group,
100 Cummings Center, Suite 265-D, Beverly, MA 01915, USA.
T (978) 282-9590 F (978) 283-2742 QuartoKnows.com

10 9 8 7 6 5 4 3 2 1

ISBN: 978-1-63159-601-8

Digital edition published in 2018

Library of Congress Cataloging-in-Publication Data available

Publisher: Corinne Roberts
Designer: David Robayo – 34 studio
Translator: Melissa McMahon
Production: Lou Playfair

Printed in China by C&C Offset Printing Co., Ltd.